D1511153

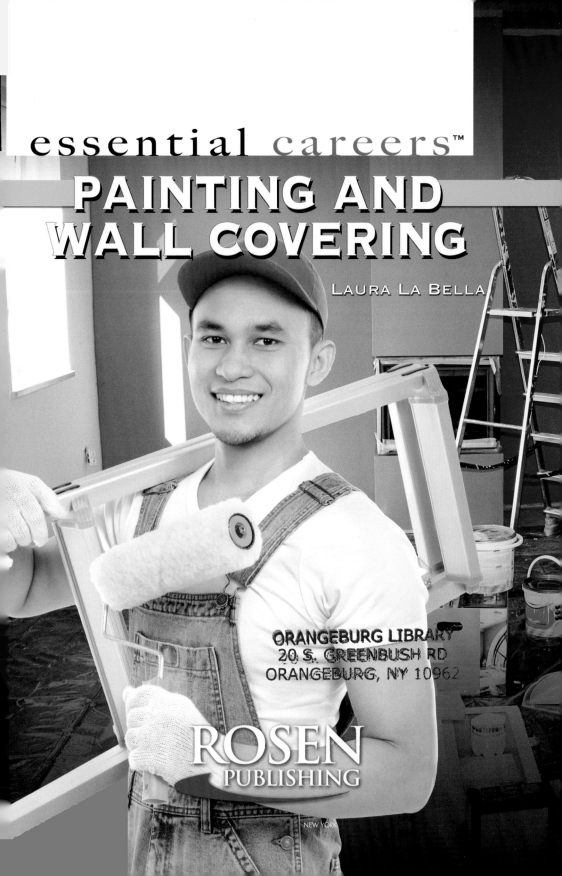

essential careers™

PAINTING AND WALL COVERING

Laura La Bella

ROSEN
PUBLISHING

NEW YORK

Published in 2016 by The Rosen Publishing Group, Inc.

29 East 21st Street, New York, NY 10010

Library of Congress CataloginginPublication Data

La Bella, Laura, author.
 Careers in painting and wall covering / Laura La Bella. -- First edition.
     pages cm. -- (Essential careers)
 Includes bibliographical references and index.
 ISBN 978-1-4994-6219-7 (library bound)
 1. House painting--Vocational guidance--Juvenile literature. 2. Paperhanging--Vocational guidance--Juvenile literature. 3. House painters--Juvenile literature. 4. Paperhangers--Juvenile literature. I. Title. II. Series: Essential careers.
 TT320.L23 2016
 698.1023--dc23

Manufactured in the United States of America.

contents

INTRO

DUCTION

The work of painters and wall coverers is around us everywhere. From the most common painting projects, such as the interiors and exteriors of homes, fences, bridges, and buildings, to unusual painting endeavors, such as intricate murals on the sides of public buildings to custom-painted projects such as airplanes decked out with bright colors and cartoon characters. In the same realm are wall coverers, whose main job is to take a blank slate of drywall and give it personality via traditional and nontraditional wall coverings, such as wallpaper or various types of fabrics, metals, or other textiles. Both painting and wall covering are skilled, highly artistic, and creative jobs.

They are also career fields that are very much in demand.

Covering both residential and commercial projects, the work of painters and wall coverers is done by people who work at large construction companies, at small custom-design firms, and also at independent, privately owned businesses. Painters can specialize in exterior painting, where they may be experts in painting architectural structures, such as bridges or public memorials, as well as other large commercial projects. They may choose to specialize in interior painting, where they may use a wide variety of painting techniques to create different textures or decorative finishes and effects on the walls inside of a home. Wall coverers may be experts in putting up wallpaper, or they may specialize in installing custom-made wall coverings that can range from soundproof tiles and decorative fabric inlays to wood, steel, tin, or other materials used to create a desired effect on wall surfaces or even ceilings. They are also responsible for specialized stucco finishes used as sculptural or artistic material in various kinds of architecture, from homes and churches to businesses.

According to *U.S. News & World Report*'s list of "Best Construction Jobs," careers in painting are among the best jobs in the construction industry based on strong job growth, a healthy salary, a good employment rate, a low stress level, and a solid work-life balance. Jobs for wall coverers, a career field listed under a larger category of building finishing contractors by the US Bureau of Labor Statistics (BLS), are also on the rise because of the increased interest in creating new and different wall treatments in homes or in installing custom-design work for specialty home or business projects.

In 2012, the latest year figures are available from the US Bureau of Labor Statistics, painters held 316,200 jobs in the United States. These are jobs in which companies employed painters or an individual has owned his or her own painting company. This number doesn't account for people who may provide painting or wall-covering services on the side as a part-time job while being employed at a full-time job in a related or even an unrelated career.

What makes a career in painting and wall covering attractive is the flexibility in the type of work you may do and the creativity you have to take a space, whether it's a single wall, a building complex, or a bridge that spans a river, and make it look good, whether it is a restoration, new construction, or even creating a beautiful piece of art.

chapter 1

CAREERS IN PAINTING AND WALL COVERING

The United States Capitol is a symbol of American democracy. Located in Washington, DC, it is a significant government building, housing the legislative branch of the US federal government. The US Capitol dome, which sits above the US Capitol, is world-renowned as one of the most recognizable pieces of architecture in the United States. Built of cast iron more than 150 years ago,

Skilled painters are required to repair and restore historical landmarks such as the US Capitol building.

the dome had not been restored since 1960. In January 2014, a multiyear restoration project to fix the dome began. Included in this work is paint abatement, which is the process of safely reducing or removing lead paint, priming the repaired dome surface, and then finally repainting the dome in protective and weather-resistant paint. Performing all of this work are skilled painters.

A Wide Range of Careers in Painting and Wall Covering

Careers in painting and wall covering can include a wide range of both residential and commercial projects. Residential projects are those jobs performed at private homes, such as painting or installing wallpaper or other textural wall coverings in any room in a home. Commercial projects are painting or wall-covering jobs that occur at a business or other spaces used by the public, such as office buildings, government buildings, schools, churches, or shopping centers.

What Do Painters Do?

Whether it's a type of building or structural entity such as a bridge, handrail, or fence, painters are needed to enhance the interior and exterior look of these structures. But painters do more than just brush a coat of paint on a surface. Professional painters begin by preparing work surfaces. This may mean that a painter will have to remove old finishes by stripping, sanding, wire brushing, burning, or using water or abrasive blasting. Then they need to take care of the surface by filling cracks, holes, and joints or repairing any other types of damage to the work surface. Next, they smooth the surface using sandpaper, scrapers, brushes, or sanding machines and treat surfaces for protection against mold, water damage, or other

Outdoor paint jobs may require workers to erect scaffolding in order to reach difficult places.

environmental issues, all of that before they begin to paint. The paint has to be put on in a way that ensures the finish adheres properly, which may include applying primers or sealers to secure the coating.

Painters use a wide range of brushes, spray guns, or rollers and are knowledgeable about which equipment provides the desired result. Painters must cover surfaces, such as floors, furniture, or windows, to protect them during painting. For outdoor projects, painters may need to erect scaffolding or ladders for work that takes place above ground level.

Painters also read work orders or receive instructions from supervisors or homeowners to determine work requirements, project guidelines, and the amount and type of materials needed. They select and purchase tools or finishes for surfaces to be covered, considering durability, ease of handling, methods of application, and customers' wishes. Finally, painters perform any special details such as stenciling, decorations, or special finishing techniques like sponging, ragging, layering, or faux finishing.

WHAT DO WALL COVERERS DO?

Wall coverings are used to brighten a dark room, make a space feel larger, create a desired atmosphere, or add personality to a space. Wall coverings can give a room character, set a theme, or simply make a space more interesting.

Wall coverings can vary greatly depending on what a customer wants or needs in a particular space. Most commonly associated with putting up wallpaper, skilled wall coverers can do more than add a floral pattern to your kitchen wall or place a brightly colored border along the edge of the ceiling in the bedroom. They can install wall upholstery, which is when fabrics are used to cover all or part of a wall; install wall graphics, which are custom-created stickers, designs, or decals applied to a wall for decoration; install wall panel systems to control or augment sound in a home, theater, or other building; and install special items, such as large-scale dry-erase boards for schools or custom-made acoustical panels for recording studios. Wall coverers are also responsible for the stucco finish used as a sculptural and artistic material in architecture. Wall coverers perform a number of tasks as part of their jobs— among them, they choose wallpaper or other wall coverings such as vinyl, metals, and textiles; remove old wall coverings and repair any damage to the surface of the wall; install wall graphics, or large-scale images, onto a wall surface; determine the size of the space to estimate how much material is needed

TYPES OF DECORATIVE PAINTING TECHNIQUES

Decorative painting techniques allow for more than just washing a wall, floor, or other surface in a solid color of paint. They enable painters to give a more interesting look to the surface or even give the illusion of wood grain, stone, metal, or textiles like linen or leather. Some popular decorative painting techniques include:

Chalkboard paint—A style in which you create a surface that can be written on with chalk. There are several different colors of this type of paint.

Checkerboard—An inexpensive way to create the look of a checkerboard marble floor on the surface of a floor.

Color washing—Using paint and a glaze, color washing adds dimension to paint and bathes a wall in various tones of the same color.

Dry-brushing—A technique in which the walls are painted in a way that leaves visible brush strokes as means of decoration.

Fresco—Using latex paint and glazes, a fresco finish is a mottled, parchment look on a wall surface.

Geometric reflections—Decorative elements, geometric shapes that overlap each other, can highlight a room and give some life to a blank wall.

Glitter—The glitter effect, which uses tiny specks of reflective materials mixed into the paint used to finish the wall, adds sparkle to a wall surface.

Ragging—Using old wadded rags dipped in a glaze finish, ragging can give the appearance of shifting shades of color. It can also create a look of work leather or of soft, faded denim.

Smooshing—This technique is used to imitate the look of marble on a surface.

Sponging—Among the easiest techniques to learn and perfect, sponging uses a sponge dipped in glaze and then pressed randomly on a wall to create a mottled look.

Strié—Using a strié brush, this technique creates a soft, natural, striped texture on a wall.

Washed stripes—This technique creates stripes of varying widths of paint on your walls. The stripes can be different colors or different widths, or they can be the same color and one common width throughout the wall space.

for a particular project; read and interpret design or architectural plans to understand the scope and parameters of a project; and repair any damage to a wall covering or touch up a custom-made upholstery job when needed.

WORK ENVIRONMENT

Painters and wall coverers work in a wide range of environments and locations. They can work inside homes, businesses, or other commercial structures, or they can work outside painting or installing coverings on the exteriors of buildings, homes, or structures such as bridges, fences, and railings.

Most painters who work on industrial or infrastructure projects, such as bridges or murals on the sides of buildings, almost always work outside in dry, warm weather. This means jobs are finished as weather permits. If it rains, no work can be accomplished, and the painter is not paid for that day's work. Those who paint bridges or buildings may be exposed to extreme heights and uncomfortable positions, and they may be required to work high up on scaffolding that is erected so a painter can reach the highest points of a building.

TYPES OF WALL COVERINGS

Wall coverings are a great way to add texture or creativity to your walls. Most common is wallpaper, which has been in use since the 1700s. Today's wall coverers can include a wide variety of materials to achieve different looks or effects, such as sound proofing.

Wallpaper can come in a variety of paper-based materials such as woodchip paper, which is particle wood between several layers of paper. It's easily hung but must be painted after installation. There is also washable wallpaper, printed with a special glaze that enables it to be wiped clean. Cork-faced wallpaper is wallpaper that includes a thin layer of cork on its surface. It creates a wood-like effect but is less expensive than paneling. Relief wallpaper has a pattern on it that hides minor imperfections in the surface of the wall.

Ceramic wall tiles are tiles that can have a matte finish (no shine) or can have a reflective shine from a glaze that is coated on top of each tile. They are applied to walls with an adhesive material such as mortar, which makes them stick to a surface. Grout is used in between tiles. Tile is easily cleaned, very durable, and waterproof.

Grass cloth wall covering is made from grass that has been woven into a mat that is glued to paper backing. This wall covering is very sustainable, or environmentally friendly, but it is also fragile and can be damaged easily.

Paneling is used to cover up walls in poor condition or for a woodlike effect that is less expensive than using real wood. Paneling is nailed or glued to wall surfaces.

Fabric tiles are often used for a specific purpose, such as sound-proofing. Fabric tiles are squares of fabric that are affixed to walls, ceilings, and doors.

Upholstery is made with fabrics or other materials such as linen, textiles, or leather that are affixed to walls to achieve a desired look.

The tools of wall covering include a wide metal putty knife and a sharp blade to cut off excess paper such as the ones shown here.

PHYSICALLY DEMANDING WORK

Painting and wall coverers encounter many physical demands. This job requires an excessive amount of climbing, bending, kneeling, and stretching to paint or cover hard to reach areas. Equipment needs to be moved into and out of work areas on a daily basis. This can include carrying heavy paint cans, steel or metal ladders and scaffolding, and cases of tools that vary in size. These kinds of jobs often require long hours on your feet standing to measure, assess, repair and prepare various surfaces before the main work of painting or installing a wall covering begins.

A job as a wall coverer and painter can be demanding on your body.
It can also be dangerous.

HIGH RATE OF INJURY

Because painting and wall covering is a physically demanding job, it comes with a high rate of injury. Common injuries suffered by painters and wall coverers include falls from ladders or scaffolding, muscle pulls and strains from heavy lifting or maneuvering of equipment, knee or leg injuries from excessive kneeling and standing, and shoulder and neck injuries from looking or stretching upward to reach high edges or corners of walls and structures.

A LOW STRESS JOB

While painters and wall coverers must adhere to deadlines to finish a job on time, most workers report that there are few other stressors to the job. One other main source of stress can be if the client changes his or her mind about the project or is unhappy about the result. In larger companies, a project manager handles these situations, but in smaller ones, the workers themselves must deal with clients to ensure that they are happy.

SALARY AND COMPENSATION

According to the latest available numbers from the Bureau of Labor Statistics, the median annual wage for construction and maintenance painters was $35,190 in May 2012. The top 10 percent earned more than $60,240 annually in the profession. Painters or wall coverers who specialize in painting structures, such as bridges, or in the installation of custom-made wall coverings tend to have higher wages.

A challenge for painters, in particular those who work outdoors, is the fluctuation in work throughout the calendar year. For those who work in the Midwest or the Northeast, which experience several months of winter weather, weather is a factor in being able to work on a daily basis, so learning to budget money is important when you do not have a regular monthly or bimonthly paycheck arriving in your mailbox. Often, painters in areas of the country where there are weather extremes work seasonally and are employed in a different line of work in the off-season. Some painters also try to schedule jobs so interior work can be accomplished during colder or wetter months while outside work can be the focus during dry, warmer months.

chapter 2

THE SKILLS YOU NEED AND HOW TO GET THEM

While there are no specific qualifications such as a college degree or certification that are required to work as a general painter or wall coverer, both careers include a certain amount of on-site experience that provides the range of skills that need to be mastered if a job is to be done correctly. Most painting or wall-covering techniques can be learned through practice However, depending on your career goals and how specialized you want to be as a painter or wall coverer, you may also need to get certification or even a degree.

GENERAL BUILDING AND CONSTRUCTION KNOWLEDGE

In general, painters and wall coverers should have general building and construction knowledge, including an understanding of any local building codes related to painting, wall coverings, and their associated products. For example, in 1977, the United States banned the use of lead-based paint after it was found to cause a wide variety of health issues in people who lived in homes that had interior spaces painted with lead paint. Removing lead paint requires specialized knowledge, specific required safety precautions, and permits issued by local or state

Painters and wall coverers need building and construction knowledge to adhere to building codes and safety requirements.

building code offices. In larger construction companies, it is the company's responsibility to get the permits needed before a project begins, but individuals or smaller companies must get these themselves, which may mean dealing with state or local government before starting a job.

Some jobs require government-regulated specialized training.

LEAD PAINT ABATEMENT SPECIALISTS

Lead paint abatement is the process of safely reducing or removing lead paint from homes and businesses. Lead paint abatement specialists, and the firms they work for, must be certified to remove lead paint. It is very dangerous to the people in the nearby environment if lead paint is removed improperly, and in many instances it can cause higher risk than if lead paint is left unattended. To become a lead paint abatement specialist you must be certified by the EPA, or Environmental Protection Agency, which regulates the training and certification process for lead pain abatement specialists in the United States. The course is a minimum of eight hours and includes information on why lead paint is bad, health concerns related to lead paint, regulations for removal, assessing a lead paint removal project, containing lead paint dust during the removal process, cleaning and checking your work after removal, and accurate record keeping and documentation. The EPA's website (www.leadcertificationnyc.com) has more details on becoming certified in lead paint abatement.

Painters and wall coverers should have the following skills:

Good time-management skills—Since painters and wall coverers are contracted to do work by customers, it's essential that they manage their time appropriately for a number of reasons. First, work should be completed in a reasonable amount of time to accommodate a customer's deadline. Second, to continue to schedule projects and make money, painters need to be efficient and productive so they can accomplish as many jobs as possible to satisfy demand for their services. Third, since reputation is a key factor in repeat business in construction-related projects, completing a project on time, within budget, and correctly can lead to positive reviews and referrals by customers.

Supervisory or management skills—For those painters or wall coverers in management positions who have workers reporting to them, its essential to have strong skills when overseeing personnel. Managers can mediate an issue between a worker and a client, clarify the scope of the job, and manage and prioritize jobs for staff.

Critical-thinking skills to solve problems—Advanced experience as a painter or wall coverer means you have the skills to think critically and suggest ways to solve a problem. You can also make recommendations to customers on the best products or techniques to use to achieve a desired result.

Coordination for working in tight or awkward spaces—Being physically fit is essential to reaching and working in tight, awkward, or uncomfortable spaces.

Decision-making skills for deciding the best approach to a particular project—A project may be able to be solved in multiple ways, but which direction is best in terms of time management and cost? Strong decision-making skills help you when you need to weigh a range of options to determine which approach is best given a certain project.

Attention to detail—A bad paint job can stand out, so being attentive to detail and being precise is important, especially since the work of a painter or wall coverer is more immediately recognizable than the work that goes into a construction job. You might not know if a beam is positioned correctly in the ceiling, but if a paint job is messy, if the edges are sloppy, or if wall paper is hung unevenly or has bubbles under the surface, someone will notice right away.

Dependability—Showing up at the scheduled time, completing a job on time, and adhering to an established budget are all signs of dependability.

EDUCATION

For painters and wall coverers who are employed by construction companies or private firms, the minimum educational requirement needed is a high school diploma or a GED, which stands for General Educational Development. This test is administered by your state and takes the place of a high school diploma for those who have not or cannot complete a structured school-based program. For those who go into business for themselves, they need no formal educational requirement.

There are a number of educational pathways you can take to learn the skills needed to become a painter or wall coverer. Based on your career goals and aspirations, you can complete a vocational program designed to teach you how to become a painter or wall coverer, complete course work to earn a certificate or two-year degree to gain some basic construction industry knowledge along with trade skills in painting, or earn a four-year degree in management, business, or construction management if you wish to own or lead a construction company or design firm. If you are interested in more specialized design skills, then you might want to pursue a degree in interior design or decorating. Each pathway has specific requirements. Choosing one depends on your career goals.

VOCATIONAL TRAINING PROGRAMS

Vocational training programs include roughly two hundred to three hundred hours of class work where students learn technical skills as they build in class work toward more advanced trade or vocational concepts. A wide range of skills and knowledge can be gathered through training courses that cover topics such as safety, working with chemicals, materials handling, basic industrial math, practical measurements, hand and power tools, painting, painting techniques, plastering, and wallpapering. Courses range in duration, but most are five hours or shorter. Vocational programs are offered online and on site at vocational schools and are often flexible to accommodate adult learners who may be learning a trade while working full- or part-time in a related or nonrelated job. Vocational programs often do not have any admission requirements, and they tend to be the least expensive educational option.

TWO-YEAR DEGREE PROGRAMS

Often offered at technical schools or community colleges, two-year degree programs offer an associate's degree or a certificate in industrial painting, drywalling, or decorating. An associate's degree is a two-year program, or a minimum of sixty credit hours in construction trade–related courses in painting, drywalling, drywall finishing, glazing, filing compounds and procedures, wall preparation and repair, wall covering, and decorating; general building industry courses, such as building safety and construction technology, foreman training, safe work practices, construction materials, computer aided drafting, general business, occupational safety and health, and business computing; plus courses in general liberal arts, such as writing, algebra, communication, math, and basic science.

In a certificate program, students complete sixteen to

twenty-four credit hours in a program designed to provide introductory knowledge and skills in the industrial painting, drywalling, or wall-covering trades. Courses may include topics such as basic painting, decorating and decorative painting, abrasive blasting techniques, color mixing, wood finishing, non-painting decorative finishes, filling compounds and procedures, ladders and scaffolding, understanding basic blueprints, and spray painting/coatings and coverings. Often students who complete a certificate program are prepared to become entry-level apprentices under skilled and experienced painters or wall coverers. Certificate programs are also available in general contracting management or construction management, where students learn the fundaments of running a construction business, from managing construction projects and construction personnel to common practices in the industry. Coursework can include topics such as construction project scheduling, construction technology, management and supervision, construction law, preconstruction estimating, risk management, green and sustainable building practices, and facilities management.

Two-year degree programs and certificate programs often have some basic admission requirements, which include a high school diploma or GED, transcripts from any previously completed college-level courses, and an application for enrollment. Tuition for certificate programs and two-years programs varies depending on the school or program you choose to attend. These programs are more expensive than vocational programs but less expensive than a four-year bachelor's degree program.

FOUR-YEAR DEGREE PROGRAMS

For students who wish to become managers or owners of a construction business, custom-design firm, or small paint specialty business, a four-year degree program in business, management or construction management can provide you with the knowledge you need to operate and manage a construction business or prepare you for a leadership position in the construction industry. A four-year degree in business or a related topic is helpful if you decide to open your own

A business degree is helpful if you want to own or run a business that specializes in painting or wall covering.

business. These programs are often 120 to 140 credit hours. The curriculum includes construction-trade courses such as construction graphics, woodworking and masonry, concrete and steel, and construction surveying; fundamental construction industry topics such as environmental science for construction management, structural design, building codes and zoning, construction law, mechanical and electrical equipment, construction cost analysis, and specifications; as well as business-management courses like organizational behavior, finance and financial accounting, value management, macro- and micro-economics, operations management, and management skills.

Admission requirements vary for four-year programs based on the program and school you choose to attend. At minimum, an applicant needs to have a specific high school grade-point average and have completed courses in math, science, English, and

Certificates may be necessary to show that you have the skills and training to do highly specialized work.

social studies. Four-year degree programs are the most expensive educational pathway; however, they also present a wider range of career options if your aspirations include management, leadership, or ownership of a construction, painting, or wall-covering business.

GET CERTIFIED

For painters and wall coverers, certifications are available in highly specific areas of the industry. These certificates show that you have completed the necessary course work or that you have documented experience in a particular area of painting or wall covering.

NACE International, formerly known as the National Association of Corrosion Engineers, offers certifications for professionals who use coatings to protect the corrosion of certain building materials such as bridges or marine/maritime materials. According to the NACE website (www.naceinstitute. org), specific certifications are for those individuals who are experienced, knowledgeable, and capable of performing work at an advanced level with certain types of materials with high rates of corrosion. The most common certification for construction painters is called protective coating specialist. At minimum this certification requires a high school diploma, twelve years of work experience in protective coatings, and the successful completion of NACE's Protective Coatings Exam. Certification can also be achieved for applicants with less than twelve years of experience if they have completed certain training courses in protective coatings.

chapter 3

APPRENTICESHIPS: LEARN BY DOING

While there are a variety of courses you can take to learn the basic skills associated with painting and wall covering, typically the skills you need are learned on the job. Many employers seek painters and wall coverers that have participated in an apprenticeship program. Some painters and wall coverers enroll in formal training programs at vocational and technical schools or at community colleges. But an apprenticeship program differs from these in that it combines classroom instruction with on-the-job training.

WHAT IS AN APPRENTICESHIP?

An apprentice is someone with little to no training who is paired with an experienced, master-level craftsman who teaches a novice everything he or she needs to know about the craft. A painting or wall-covering apprentice learns about tools and tool selection, equipment, wall-covering application techniques, different types of paint and paint finishes, wall repair, surface preparation, blueprint interpretation, and various safety procedures. Apprenticeship programs educate novice painters or wall coverers in all aspects of the craft until they are prepared to work on their own with little to no guidance. Apprenticeship

In an apprenticeship, the apprentice works side-by-side with a master to learn the tools and techniques of the trade.

programs can take two to five years to complete.

As an apprentice, you will receive paid on-the-job training. Most programs require a minimum of 144 hours of technical instruction (classroom course work) and 2,000 hours of paid, on-the-job training with a master-level craftsman.

All of the aspects of painting and wall covering, including preparing the area where you will work, are important to the finished product.

Why You Should Take That Summer Job Seriously

Your summer job could be a stepping-stone to a major career. Many students take a summer job to save money toward schooling costs or for expenses they incur as a high school or college student. But that summer job may be more than just a few dollars in the bank. A job as a painter or an assistant to a wall coverer or another construction position allows you to learn about the construction industry firsthand as you develop skills you can't obtain in a classroom. Among those skills are two that are in demand by today's employers: effective communication skills and real-world critical-thinking skills. A 2014 *Forbes* article titled "The Two Key Traits Employers Need from Today's College Graduates," by Robert Farrington, outlines why these two traits are key. He wrote: "No matter how high your GPA, or whether you graduated with honors, if you can't communicate clearly in an interview and demonstrate that you can solve a real world business problem, employers will not want to hire you." Having real-world experience on your résumé also helps you stand out to future employers and gives you an advantage if you are applying to apprenticeship programs in painting and wall covering. In addition, summer jobs in the construction industry can also help you network with professionals who may be interested in hiring you once you complete your educational program or who can provide references about your work to others.

TECHNOLOGY AND PAINTING

Technological advances in chemical development have impacted the painting industry in a powerful way. Dow Chemical, a leading chemical corporation, has been developing coating materials that are designed to improve the performance of sealers, primers, paint, glazes, and other finishing products used on architectural and industrial painting and wall-covering projects. These chemical coating materials lengthen the life of products used on surfaces by making them more resistant to wear, changes in temperature or extreme weather conditions, and sun exposure and damage caused by the sun's ultraviolet rays, while also helping them seal and protect surfaces better. They also help some surfaces that are more resistant to holding paint.

Large-scale industrial jobs sometimes require advanced technology and special training to complete.

WHAT WILL I LEARN AS AN APPRENTICE?

As an apprentice you will complete a range of classes that cover topics such as the types and varieties of wall coverings, the types of paints and paint finishes, how and when to use coatings, erecting scaffolding and using ladders for jobs above ground level, lead regulations and awareness, how to mix color, and how to work in confined spaces.

Painters and wall coverers use a range of chemicals in their daily work. Some of these chemicals have specific safety regulations and require protective gear such as gloves, masks, breathing machines, or safety suits. Apprenticeship programs will educate you in the basic knowledge of chemicals and hazardous materials, how to work safely with these materials, and how to dispose of them properly and safely. You will also learn first aid and CPR.

Your coursework will also cover how to select the correct materials based on the scope of the job, which equipment you will need to utilize while on the job, and how to evaluate and prepare various types of a work surfaces (drywall, Sheetrock, metals, plaster, etc.) for painting application. You will also learn how to determine the amount of paint or wall covering you need for a project. Understanding how to properly choose and mix paint is also covered in an apprenticeship program.

As apprenticeship programs combine on-the-job training with classroom instruction, most classes are offered in the evenings, often one night per week while an apprentice works during the day. Sometimes classes may be held on the weekends.

With the construction industry using more and more technology, some apprenticeship programs include some basic computer knowledge, such as using CAD (computer-aided drafting) or other industry-specific software.

At the conclusion of your apprenticeship program you may be required to complete a written or oral exam or provide a portfolio or samples of work you completed during the program.

FINDING AN APPRENTICESHIP PROGRAM

Most apprenticeship programs require a high school diploma as the minimum educational requirement. However, you may be able to start some apprenticeship programs while you are in high school. As a preapprentice you could work summers, evenings, or weekends until you graduate from high school. Apprenticeship programs can be found online on the websites of several leading construction worker unions or professional associations such as the International Union of Painters and Allied Trades, the Signatory Painters and Contractors Association, or the Associated Builders and Contractors, Inc. Many of these organizations have local chapters throughout the country that provide apprenticeship programs, other training programs, and continuing education for current professional painters.

PROFESSIONAL WORK AND BENEFITS WHILE YOU TRAIN

As an apprentice, you will be employed as a working painter or wall coverer while you take courses. As an employee you will earn a salary and, in most cases, you will have medical benefits after a certain period of time in the program. Qualified union painters receive health, dental, and vision plans as well as pension and vacation plans.

Setting Yourself Up for Success

When you complete an apprenticeship program you become a journeyman painter or wall coverer. A journeyman painter is someone who has competed an apprenticeship program and has more than four years of work experience. Those who successfully complete apprenticeships are in the best place to position themselves for successful painting careers.

chapter 4

GETTING A JOB AS A PAINTER OR WALL COVERER

With your education now complete, you're ready to begin applying for your first job as a professional painter or wall coverer. As you begin your job search, you need to be prepared with a strategy. You should have a professional résumé that outlines your education and experience, know how to identify available painting or wall-covering positions, be prepared to talk about your accomplishments during an interview, and know how to network to build connections in the construction industry.

CRAFTING A PROFESSIONAL RÉSUMÉ

Before your job search can even begin, you need to create a well-written résumé that highlights your education, skills, abilities, and accomplishments. When applying for a job, your résumé is the first impression you can make on a potential employer. It needs to be well thought out to present your experience clearly. Your résumé is the one document that will tell a potential employer about your work experience, any education or apprenticeship programs you have completed, all of the skills you are proficient in, equipment you are able to use, the types of special painting or wall-covering techniques you are adept at

Writing a résumé can be difficult but you can get help at a local library or a state department of labor.

performing, and any other abilities you have developed up to this point.

A well-crafted résumé is organized into sections (e.g., Education, Experience, Skills, etc.), and each section should neatly and concisely outline your abilities or accomplishments within these categories. For help in creating a résumé, you can turn to the career services office of the vocational school, community college, or four-year college you attended. These offices are staffed with professionals that know how to best craft a résumé for all different types of industries. If you completed an apprenticeship program, some programs may have career services professionals to help you work on your résumé. There are also professional companies that specialize in helping people write a résumé. You can do an online search for one of these companies.

SUCCEEDING AT THE JOB SEARCH

It's exciting to search for a job. And technology has made identifying open positions in nearly every industry much easier. Today, hundreds of job search websites are available to help you identify the type of job you

HOW THE WEB CAN WORK FOR YOU

The Internet is one of the most valuable tools you can use when searching for a job. It can help you identify open positions in the construction field and enable you to research potential employers, and you can seek out advice on everything from writing a winning cover letter to topics to avoid in an interview. Follow these strategies to make the Web work for you:

Join LinkedIn: LinkedIn is a professional, career-driven networking site where people can post their accomplishments, an overview of their career, and the types of positions they may be interested in. You can also connect to other professionals, seek out their advice, or research a company and its leadership staff.

Conduct a self search: Your cyber identity could turn off a potential employer. Almost everyone has an online profile. Have you posted inappropriate photos, made controversial comments, or participated in offensive events? Hiring managers will search your name, and anything you've posted can, and most likely will, turn up. Be proactive and conduct a self search first. Clean up your online presence by deleting photos or any comments a potential employer could deem unsavory.

Promote yourself: Drive traffic to your online presence by updating your LinkedIn profile with your latest accomplishments, create a professional website that highlights your work, and use social media like Instagram to post information about your professional endeavors.

Network online: LinkedIn and other professional online networks enable you to reach out to other professionals in your field. You can connect with others in the construction field to learn about opportunities or to continue to grow in your field.

Send a thank you: A personal e-mail sent to the hiring manager or other personnel that you met with or interviewed with is an easy way to follow up after an interview. A better way to connect is by sending a handwritten note. It's much more impressive and shows you can go the extra mile.

Meeting a potential employer in person is a good way to let them get to know you and how you work.

are looking for. These sites post open positions and enable you to apply directly online. Many larger construction companies also post job openings on their company websites. Some may use industry-specific or general job search sites to announce open positions.

It can feel exhausting to search the Internet for a job. But knowing how to look and what to look for can make the process easier and produce better results.

SEARCH BY INDUSTRY

The construction industry has several general job posting websites, such as ConstructionJobs.com and SnagaJob.com. These websites are extensive databases for construction-related job postings. Both allow you to search by keyword (such as "painter" or "wall coverer") or by location if you are seeking employment in a particular state or region of the country. Some of the best construction websites are:

ConstructionJobs.com
IHireConstruction.com
CareersinConstruction.com
Jobs.Monster.com/v-construction.aspx
Indeed.com/q-Construction-jobs.html

POST YOUR RÉSUMÉ

Since employers use industry-specific websites to post jobs, they also search the database of workers who are seeking employment. By posting your résumé to one of these sites, you can reach out to a potential employer who might be searching for someone with a specific skill set.

CREATE A PROFILE

Many company websites feature career pages where you can complete a profile about your job interests, credentials, experiences, and salary requirements. If positions open up that match your profile, you may receive a notification that an opening has been posted. Sometimes a hiring manager will contact you directly.

JOIN A PROFESSIONAL ASSOCIATION

The construction industry is filled with professional organizations for nearly every type of worker, from painters and wall coverers to welders and iron workers. These professional organizations seek to connect candidates with open positions and often have a career section on their websites where you can post your résumé, search a job listing, or learn more about advanced skills that are in demand.

REGISTER FOR JOB ALERTS AND RSS FEEDS

Want to know the latest trends emerging in your industry, including job alerts and hiring notices? Sign up for job alerts and RSS feeds. RSS stands for Really Simple Syndication, which uses a family of standard web feed formats to publish information on a daily or near daily basis. If construction websites have RSS feeds they will often announce when new jobs have been added to the database, which saves you from checking each website directly every few days.

GET A FILTER

Filters weed out the information you don't want. If you're searching for painting jobs, you don't need job postings for

The more prepared you are for your interview, the less nervous you will be and the more likely you will be to get the job.

TIPS FOR A SUCCESSFUL INTERVIEW

Plan ahead. Research the company you are interviewing with to learn as much as possible about who they are and what types of construction projects they specialize in. Review your résumé. Think about each of your educational and professional experiences so you are prepared to answer questions about what you learned and how you might adapt those skills to the position you are applying for.

Make eye contact with your interviewer when you answer questions. It shows your interest in the job and in the person you're speaking with.

Be positive. Don't speak negatively about past employers or past clients. Frame all challenging experiences as learning opportunities.

Listen. Be aware of what the interviewer is saying about his or her company and the job you are interviewing for. Ask follow-up questions to show you are engaged in the conversation, listening to what is being said, and interested in the company and the job.

Prepare some questions. Ask specific questions about the job you are applying for, such as if you will be required to learn new painting or wall-covering techniques independently or if they will assist in providing training opportunities.

Focus on your achievements. In answering an interviewer's questions, try to provide information that demonstrates what you know and how you would adapt your knowledge to particular projects.

welders. Get only the information you need and want by filtering out all of the content you don't need or that doesn't apply to you or positions you qualify for.

IMPRESS AT THE INTERVIEW

Getting a job offer comes down to the interview. Your résumé may have gotten you in the door with your skills and experience, but the interview is where you can sell yourself to a potential employer.

An interview is an opportunity for you to show an employer that you can do the job and that you fit into a company's culture. It's also a chance for you to learn more about a company.

An interview should be a conversation between you and an employer about not just your skills and how you can best succeed in the company. An employer may be looking for the perfect candidate, but you need to look for the company that is right for you. An interview is the best way to

Consider all of your options if you get a job offer. If you have other interviews, ask if they can wait a day or two for your answer.

learn more about both a job and a company and see if you can picture yourself working with and for the company's team.

In an interview, you should always act professionally. Turn off your cell phone, leave gum and mints at home, avoid bringing drinks in to the interview, and make sure to dress professionally. Arrive early. If the location of the interview is unfamiliar, drive the route the day before so you know how long it will take to get there, where you'll need to park, and how to get into the building. Large companies can have multiple parking lots and numerous buildings. You don't want to be late or flustered during your first meeting with a potential employer.

Your First Job

Congratulations! You've been hired for your first painting or wall-covering job. Now the real work begins.

Your first job is an opportunity to learn from seasoned painting and wall-covering professionals, as well as the construction industry. Put yourself out there and soak up as much knowledge as you can. It's also a time where you will begin to learn a lot about the job world that you aren't able to learn in classes. While you are working at your first job, remember that your first job is just that, the first in a long line of opportunities you will have. Your first job doesn't predict the future of your career, nor does it teach you all you need to know. It's an opportunity to begin your career. You'll change jobs, maybe even career fields, over the course of your professional life.

Your attitude is as important as the work you do. One of the biggest complaints about first-time employees is that they often expect more responsibility than they are prepared for and they tend to think they know more than seasoned professionals. Your first job is a time for you to soak in as much as you can. You have to learn the ropes, prove your skills, and earn respect before you can begin to be assigned jobs with more responsibility or that require higher levels of skill.

Every company, division, department, and office has politics. Learn how decisions are made, who calls the shots, and who has influence.

Each organization has its own culture that comes through in behavior and actions. Find out what the company stands for, and learn if there are unwritten rules of etiquette.

You're in charge of your career, not your company. It used to be that a company took responsibility for moving you along a career path. Now, it's up to you to build your skills, take the initiative, and contribute to the company. The knowledge you learn will serve you well as you get promoted. Or, if you decide to leave, you'll take that knowledge and experience with you.

Don't wait for compliments. If you want to know how you are doing, ask for feedback. Schedule periodic meetings with your direct supervisors to inquire about how your work performance is perceived and if you are producing good quality work. Seek constructive criticism on how to improve and ask how you can do better. You should always have an idea of how well you are meeting your employer's expectations as well as what's expected from you.

chapter 5

THE CONSTRUCTION INDUSTRY: A GROWING CAREER FIELD

The news is good for careers in the construction industry. According to Dodge Data and Analytics, a leading construction industry forecasting and business planning company, jobs in construction are on the upswing, with growth projected in five key areas: commercial building, which includes office and office building construction; institutional building, which means K–12 schools, college campus construction projects, and health care facilities; single family housing; multifamily housing, which means homes that have multiple apartments or private residences within them; and public works, which include community buildings. A 2014 survey from the Associated General Contractors of America found that firms plan to start hiring more skilled construction workers. And the US Department of Labor predicts an overall employment growth of 2.6 percent, or 1.6 million new jobs, for painters and wall coverers through 2022. All of this means there will be ample jobs for you in painting and wall covering in the near future.

Construction jobs, including work as a wall coverer and painter, are on the rise.

US Bureau of Labor Statistics Projects Job Growth for Painters

According to the US Bureau of Labor Statistics (BLS), more than 62,600 painting jobs will be added to the painting and construction industry by 2022. This represents a growth rate of 19.8 percent, which is well above the average considering the average growth rate across all professions is currently around 11 percent.

According to its website, the BLS attributes this growth to "the relatively short life of paint on homes, as well as changing trends in color and application," and goes on to add that this "will continue to result in demand for painters. Investors who sell properties or rent them out also will require painters' services. Nonetheless, the ability of many homeowners to do the work themselves will temper employment growth somewhat. Growing demand for industrial painting will be driven by the need to

Working in this field can be artistic as well as technical.

prevent the corrosion and deterioration of many industrial structures by painting or coating them. Applying a protective coating to the inside of a steel tank, for example, can add years to its life expectancy."

PROFESSIONAL ADVANCEMENT

Ron Yarbrough, founder and president of Pro-Spec Painting, Inc., told *U.S. News & World Report* that the painting profession's focus areas are endless and that for painting professionals there is something for everyone. "I think there are tremendous opportunities for those that want to enter the painting trade. And I think that the field has so many different segments to it—all the way from infrastructure to new construction of commercial buildings and many types of decorative art and restoration." He goes on to say that the patience and dedication to do the work is all it takes to succeed. "People who are really committed to learning the trade can do well at it. If they set their goals high, they can make a really good living at it."

Painters and wall coverers begin their careers as journeyman painters. This designation is common among labor unions to identify a painter who has completed the necessary course work and supervised experience of a formal apprenticeship. Labor unions also use this designation to indicate the minimum salary this level worker should earn for his or her talents and skills.

To advance as a painter and wall coverer you can continue to improve your skills and apply for certifications in specialty areas of painting or wall coverings. For painters who work on repairing and painting maritime and naval projects, they can become certified as corrosion specialists.

With advanced skill sets and experience, a painter and wall coverer can become a supervisor or a mentor to an apprentice. Mentors are assigned an apprentice, who is enrolled in an apprenticeship program and works full-time under the supervision of a master-level painter or wall coverer. As a master-level professional, you will be in the position to share your knowledge and skills with a younger, less-experienced painter who is interested in carving a career path as a painter or wall coverer. You will oversee an apprentice, assign him or her tasks, and double-check the apprentice's work to ensure he or she is maintaining a high quality of performance. You would provide feedback to the apprentice on skills sets that need improvement or tips or techniques that can produce more efficient work.

AN ADVANCED CAREER: THE PAINTING FOREMAN

A painter foreman supervises the preparation, patching, finishing, and maintenance of all work surfaces using common procedures and techniques of the painting trade. A painter foreman also spends a good deal of time responding to requests for work, creating a daily or weekly schedule, and providing written documentation to his or her supervisors that a job was completed so a project can be billed to a client.

A foreman is in charge of a job, and in the case of a painting foreman, he or she assigns painters to specific tasks and supervises these activities; manages and provides all of the equipment, tools, and materials needed at a job site; orders the necessary materials needed for the job; supervises the preparation and mixing of necessary paints, primers, sealers, or other coatings needed; and coordinates the activities of all the painters assigned to him or her to ensure all aspects of a project are completed.

A foreman is also a highly skilled member of the construction team. He or she has years of experience, is a master at the craft, and can assist in problem solving when issues arise. Many painters or wall coverers aspire to be foremen and be in a supervisory role where they can gain leadership and management skills.

With business management experience, you can own a business or be a project leader.

STARTING YOUR OWN BUSINESS

Experienced, skilled painters or wall coverers may decide after years in the construction business to start their own business that utilizes their expertise. To start your own business you need a business plan, some level of businesses management experience, legal documents, and tools and equipment that your workers can use.

A business plan is a detailed document that outlines all of the details of a pending business. These include the type of business, its goals, its targeted customer base, a marketing plan to reach customers, the scope of work or services the business will provide, start-up costs, staffing needs and salaries, and ongoing operational needs. A business plan is a guideline for how you will operate your business. It's also a necessary document required by a bank or financial institution if you will be applying for a small business loan or other type of loan. Business loans can help cover initial start-up costs,

HOW TO APPLY FOR A SMALL BUSINESS LOAN

According to the Small Business Association, lenders all require the same information from an applicant applying for a small business loan. That information includes a loan application form, which tells a financial institution why are you applying for a loan, how the loan will be used, what assets need to be purchased and who your suppliers are, what other business debt you have and who your creditors are, who the members of your management team are and their background and experience, and your personal background.

You may also need to show lenders a résumé so that they know what your experience is as well as that of your team, especially any business or management experience.

You will certainly need a business plan. This is a document that outlines the type of business, its goals, its targeted customer base, a marketing plan to reach customers, the scope of work or services the business will provide, start-up costs, staffing needs and salaries, and ongoing operational needs.

A business credit report is essential for securing money. However, if you are not already in business, a personal credit report can tell a financial institution if you are high risk or if you are responsible with your finances and money management.

Income and tax return documents give a potential creditor a look at your past income. Financial statements, such as a balance sheet, income statement, bank statements, or documented cash flow, may be needed.

It is important to have something to use for

collateral. A bank is investing in your success as a business, but not all businesses succeed. To offset the loss of this investment, a bank might require collateral, which can be the value of personal or business property that will be used to secure a loan.

Banks will also need to see some legal documents. These can include business licenses and permits, articles of incorporation, copies of contracts you have with any vendors or suppliers, leases on property the business will use, or leases on any equipment you have rented.

If you are looking to start your own company, a well-written business plan can help you get a bank loan

provide capital for purchasing tools and equipment, provide salaries for a short amount of time, and assist in purchasing commercial real estate if you need a location to house your business.

If you have never owned your own business, some training is likely necessary so you know how to handle common business issues that may arise. This knowledge can come from formal college courses or from small business associations, which can be found in most midsized cities. These organizations offer courses or seminars on human resource management, sales and marketing, business growth, customer retention, financial aspects of business ownership, and other related topics.

Owning a business requires permits and other legal documents. You will need to decide on the structure of your business, such as whether you will be the sole proprietor, a corporation, or a limited liability company, each of which has its own definition and business structure. If you intend to hire employees you will need to apply for an Employer Identification Number and Taxpayer Identification Number from the Internal Revenue Service (IRS) so you can legally pay your staff and report their earnings to the IRS for tax purposes. Each local government also requires a business permit so you can legally operate a business within your local government. You local town hall or city hall has applications for local business permits.

As you establish your business you will also need equipment and tools so you can provide services to your customers. For painters and wall coverers these can include vehicles to travel to and from job sites; various painting equipment such as paint, sealers, primers, and coatings; brushes, rollers, drop cloths, trays, painter's tape, and caulk; industrial painting equipment such as blasters, paint sprayers, and pressure washers; scaffolding and ladders; and other related tools and supplies. You may also need business supplies such as a desk, copier or fax machine, telephones, cell phones for employees, tables and chairs for meetings, and general office supplies.

Finally, a location may be needed to house your new operation. A business loan can help you purchase a commercial property, renovate a portion of your home for an in-home business, or lease an office space.

With the job outlook for painters and wall coverers projected to grow by more than 20 percent from 2012 to 2022, which is faster than the average for all occupations, a career in this field will not only be profitable but will offer a variety of options for career variety and growth in terms of earning potential.

glossary

abatement A process of removal.

adhesive A material that makes one substance stick to another.

commercial A property for public use.

conservation Activities done to keep something historical, such as documents or a style of architecture, in good condition.

credit hours A unit of measuring educational credits.

custom Made specifically for one person based on a request.

durable The ability to stay strong over a long period of time or under harsh conditions.

exterior The outside of a structure or building.

inlay Pieces of one material, such as tile, set into another material, such as stone or wood.

interior The inside of a structure or building.

foyer The opening or entry of a building or home.

green A term for something that is environmentally friendly.

personnel Staff or workers.

portfolio A collection of images or samples of artistic or creative work.

residential A property for use as a home.

restoration The repairing of something to its original form.

risk management Understanding and evaluating the risk associated with a business decision.

sustainable A term used to describe building methods that do not destroy natural resources or further damage a fragile ecosystem.

tuition The cost of attending an educational program.

for more information

Associated Builders and Contractors Inc.
  440 1st Street NW, Suite 200
  Washington, DC 20001
  (202) 595-1505
  Website: www.abc.org
  ABC is a national construction industry trade association.

Canadian Paint and Coatings Association (CPCA)
  170 Laurier Avenue West, Suite 608
  Ottawa, ON K1P 5V5
  Canada
  (613) 231-3604
  Website: http://www.canpaint.com
The Canadian Paint and Coatings Association represents
  Canada's major paint and coating manufacturers and their
  industry suppliers and distributors.

International Union of Painters and Allied Trades
  7234 Parkway Drive
  Hanover, MD 21076
  (410) 564-5900
  Website: http://www.iupat.org
This association is an international trade association repre-
  senting union contractors engaged in painting, glass,
  glazing, drywall finishing, and floor covering.

Master Painters and Decorators Association (MPDA)
  2800 Ingleton Avenue
  Burnaby, BC V5C 6G7
  Canada

(888) 674-8937
Website: http://www.paintinfo.com/assoc/mpda
MPDA represents painting professionals across North
America and performs a wide range of services in support
of the industry.

Signatory Painting Contractors Organization
Website: http://www.spco.org
The Signatory Painting Contractors Organization is a
membership organization for commercial, industrial, and
residential painting contractors.

Wallcoverings Association
330 N. Wabash Avenue, Suite 2000
Chicago, IL 60611
(312) 321.5166
Website: http://www.wallcoverings.org
The Wallcoverings Association represents wall-covering manufacturers, distributors, and suppliers to the construction
industry. The organization also offers classes.

WEBSITES

Because of the changing nature of Internet links, Rosen
Publishing has developed an online list of websites related
to the subject of this book. This site is updated regularly.
Please use this link to access the list:

http://www.rosenlinks.com/ECAR/Paint

for further reading

Barclay, Adrian. *Construction Doodles: On-Site Scenes to Complete and Create.* Philadelphia, PA: Running Press Kids, 2015.

Deedrick, Tami, and Gail Saunders-Smith. *Construction Workers Help.* North Mankato, MN: Capstone Press, 2014.

Fatu, Claudiu. *Starting Your Career as a Contractor: How to Build and Run a Construction Business.* New York, NY: Allworth Press, 2015.

Ferguson's Careers in Focus: Construction. New York, NY: Ferguson Publishing, 2010.

Gisler, Margaret. *Careers for Hard Hats and Other Construction Types.* New York, NY: McGraw-Hill Education, 2008.

Heos, Bridget, and Mike Moran. *Let's Meet a Construction Worker.* Brookfield, CT: Millbrook Press Trade, 2013.

Jackson, Barbara J. *Construction Management Jumpstart.* Hoboken, NJ: Sybex/Wiley, 2010.

Kibert, Charles J. *Sustainable Construction: Green Building Design and Delivery.* Hoboken, NJ: Wiley, 2012.

Kruger, Abe, and Carl Seville. *Green Building: Principles and*

Practice in Residential Construction. Independence, KY: Cengage Learning, 2012.

La Bella, Laura. *Internships and Volunteer Opportunities for People Who Love to Build Things.* New York, NY: Rosen Publishing Group, 2012.

Leavitt, Amie Jane. *The Vo-Tech Track to Success in Architecture and Construction.* New York, NY: Rosen Publishing Group, 2014.

Metzler, Lynn, and Carrie Eko-Burgess. *The Construction Crew.* New York, NY: Henry Holt and Co./Macmillion, 2011.

Miller, Reagan. *Engineering in our Everyday Lives.* New York, NY: Crabtree Publishing Company, 2014.

Niver, Heather Moore. *Careers in Construction.* New York, NY: Rosen Publishing Group, 2013.

Reed, Bill. *The Integrative Design Guide to Green Building: Redefining the Practice of Sustainability.* Hoboken, NJ: Wiley, 2009.

Senker, Cath. *In the Workplace: Construction Careers.* Mankato, MN: Amicus, 2010.

Sneddon, Robert. *Environmental Engineering and the Science of Sustainability.* New York, NY: Crabtree Publishing Company, 2014.

Sutton, Sally. *Construction.* Somerville, MA: Candlewick Press, 2014.

Sutton, Sally. *Demolition.* Somerville, MA: Candlewick Press, 2012.

Wing, Charlie. *The Visual Handbook of Building and Remodeling.* Newtown, CT: Taunton Press, Inc., 2009.

Wolny, Philip. *Getting a Job in Building Maintenance.* New York, NY: Rosen Publishing Group, 2013.

bibliography

Architect of the Capitol. "Capital Dome Restoration Project: What It Takes." Retrieved May 18, 2015 (http://www.aoc.gov/capitol-dome-restoration-what-it-takes).

Architect of the Capitol. "Dome Restoration Project Overview." Retrieved May 18, 2015 (http://www.aoc.gov/dome/project-overview).

Benjamin Moore. "Faux and Decorative Painting Techniques." Retrieved May 18, 2015 (http://www.benjaminmoore.com/en-us/for-your-home/faux-and-decorative-finishes).

Bureau of Labor Statistics. "Painters, Construction and Maintenance: Job Outlook." Retrieved May 20, 2015 (http://www.bls.gov/ooh/construction-and-extraction/painters-construction-and-maintenance.htm#tab-6).

Cuyahoga Community College. "Associate of Applied Science Degree in Applied Industrial Technology with a Concentration in Painting." Retrieved May 20, 2015 (http://www.curricunet.com/Cuyahoga/reports/grad_reqs.cfm?programs_id=900).

EPA Lead Certification of New York. "EPA Lead Renovators Certification Initial." Retrieved May 18, 2015 (http://www.leadcertificationnyc.com/registration?eid=98310&link=BTN).

Maricopa Community Colleges. "AAS Program in

Construction Trades: Painting and Drywalling." Retrieved May 18, 2015 (https://aztransmac2.asu.edu/cgi-bin/WebObjects/acres.woa/wa/freeForm3?id=45475).

Maricopa Community Colleges. "Certificate Program in Construction Trades: Painting and Drywalling." Retrieved May 18, 2015 (https://aztransmac2.asu.edu/cgi-bin/WebObjects/acres.woa/wa/freeForm?id=45473).

McKay, Matt. "What Do I Need to Start My Own Painting Company?" *Houston Chronicle*. Retrieved May 17, 2015 (http://smallbusiness.chron.com/need-start-own-painting-company-2259.html).

McMullen, Laura. "Why You Should Take That Summer Job Seriously." *U.S. News & World Report*, May 28, 2015. Retrieved May 29, 2015 (http://money.usnews.com/money/careers/articles/2015/05/28/why-you-should-take-that-summer-job-seriously?int=b67f0a&int=b8e90a).

Sexton, Timothy. "Wall Covering Types." eHow.com. Retrieved May 18, 2015. (http://www.ehow.com/list_6538802_wall-covering-types.html)

Small Business Council of Rochester. "SBC Programs." Retrieved May 25, 2015 (https://www.rochestersbc.com/sbc-programs).

UC Berkeley Extension. "Certificate Program in Construction Management." Retrieved May 19, 2015 (http://extension.berkeley.edu/cert/const.html).

U.S. News & World Report. "How U.S. News Ranks to Best Jobs." January 13, 2015. Retrieved May 18, 2015 (http://

money.usnews.com/money/careers/articles/2014/01/22/
about-the-us-news-best-jobs-ranking-methodology).

US Small Business Administration. "Business Loan
Application Checklist." Retrieved May 25, 2015 (https://
www.sba.gov/content/business-loan-application-checklist).

index

A

apprenticeships
  benefits of, 39, 40
  how to find, 39
  what apprentices learn, 38–39
  what they are, 27, 32–34, 41, 43,
    58, 59
Associated Builders and
    Contractors, Inc., 39
associate's degree, 26

B

building codes, 20, 22
business
  how to start your own, 61–65
business plans
  how to create, 61, 62

C

career services office, 43
ceramic tiles, 14
certificate programs, 25, 26–27
certifications, 31
chalkboard paint, 12
checkerboard, 12
college
  four-year degrees, 20, 25, 27–31,
    43

commercial projects
  what they are, 9
community college, 26, 32, 43
computer skills, 38
cork-faced wallpaper, 14

D

decision-making skills, 24
decorative painting techniques
  types of, 12–13
denim
  painting techniques that look like,
    12
dependability
  importance of being reliable, 25
detail
  importance of being detail-ori-
    ented, 24–25
detailing, 11
Dow Chemical, 36
dry-brushing, 12

E

Environmental Protection Agency,
  23

F

fabric tiles, 15

76

About the Author

Laura La Bella is a writer and the author of more than twenty-five nonfiction children's books. She has repainted nearly every room in her home in a wide range of rich caramels, greens, yellows, and reds to invoke the feel of Tuscany, Italy, where her family originates. La Bella lives in Rochester, New York, with her husband and two sons.

Photo Credits

Cover, p. 1 (figure) Odua Images/Shutterstock.com; cover, p. 1 (background) tkemot/Shutterstock.com; pp. 4-5 © iStockphoto.com/Eillen; p. 8 FrozenShutter/iStock/Thinkstock; p. 10 © iStockphoto.com/dsharpie; pp. 14-15, 34-35 © iStockphoto.com/Jodi Jacobson; pp. 16-17 © iStockphoto.com/Terry J Alcorn; p. 21 © iStock.com/sturti; pp. 22-23 Maudib/iStock/Thinkstock; pp. 28-29 © iStockphoto.com/monkeybusinessimages; p. 30 © iStockphoto.com/pressdigital; p. 33 © iStockphoto.com/Necip Yanmaz; pp. 36-37 © iStockphoto.com/deemac; pp. 42-43 © iStockphoto.com/andresr; pp. 44-45 © iStockphotphoto.com/Imagesbybarbara; p. 48 © iStockphoto.com/Susan Chiang; pp. 50-51 © iStockphoto.com/4774344sean; pp. 54-55 © iStockphoto.com/Spiderstock; pp. 56-57 Zoonar RF/Thinkstock; pp. 60-61 © iStockphoto.com/zoranm; pp. 62-63 Creatas/Thinkstock

Designer: Matt Cauli; Editor/Photo Researcher: Tracey Baptiste